Canning and Preserving Food for Beginners

Essential Cookbook on How to Can and Preserve Everything in Jars with Homemade Recipes for Pressure Canning

Kaitlyn Donnelly

Disclaimer

The recipes and information in this book are provided for educational purposes only. Please always consult a licensed professional before making changes to your lifestyle or diet. The author and publisher shall have neither liability nor responsibility to anyone with respect to any loss or damage caused or alleged to be caused directly or indirectly by the information contained in this book. All trademarks and brands within this book are for clarifying purposes only and are owned by the owners themselves, not affiliated with this document.

Images from shutterstock.com

CONTENTS

INTRODUCTION 6

CHAPTER 1. Canning Basics 7

General Canning Methods 7
Canning Equipment 8
Preparing Food 10
Store Home-Canned Foods Safely 11
Good Things to Know about Syrup 11
Frequently Asked Questions 12

CHAPTER 2. Canning Fruit and Vegetables 15

Equipment Preparation 15
Packing Jars 15
General Processing 16
Canning Tomatoes 17
Preparing jams, butters, marmalades, and jellies 17

CHAPTER 3. Recipes 18

JAM and JELLY 18

Apricot Amaretto Jam 18
Raspberry Peach Jam 19
Blueberry Cinnamon Jam 20
Carrot Pineapple Pear Jam 21
Green Tomato Jam 22
Pineapple Rhubarb Jam 23
Plum Orange Jam 24
Ginger Pear Freezer Jam 25
Pina Colada Zucchini Jam 26
Strawberry Freezer Jam 27
Caramel Apple Jam 28
Christmas Cranberry Jam 29
Candy Apple Jelly 30
Lime Mint Jelly 31
Watermelon Jelly 32
Cucumber Jelly 33

SWEET TREATS 34

Plum Cranberry Walnut Conserve 34
Glazed Carrots 35
Lemon Marmalade 36
Raisin Pear Chutney 37
Chunky Peach Spread 38
Apple-Walnut Maple Confiture 39
Spicy Roasted Beet Marmalade 40
Spiced Cran-Apple and Grape Confiture 41
Rhubarb Cherry Chutney 42

Tomato Lemon Confiture..43

TOMATO TREATS **44**

Canned Zucchini Salad..44
Autumn Pepper Salsa..45
Peach Chili Sauce 46
Pungent Tomato Pear Chutney 47
Fresh-Tasting Ketchup...48
Piquant Chunky Salsa 49
Peach Salsa 50
Grandma's Favourite Salsa 51
Spaghetti Sauce 52
Green Tomato Salsa 53
Spicy Carrot Hot Sauce 54
Mild Jalapeno Tomato Salsa 55

PICLED TREATS **56**

Pickled Ginger Peaches 56
Watermelon Rind Pickles 57
Pickled Colorful Swiss Chard 58
Sandwich Topper Pickled Garlic 59
Chily Dill Pickles 60
Bread and Butter Pickles...61
Sweet Pickles 62
Pickled Brussels Sprouts 63
Pickled Green Beans 64
Christmas Pickled Morsels..65
Pickled Sweet Banana Peppers 66
Tangy Pickled Mushrooms..67
Flavor-Packed Pickled Red Grapes.......................................68
Pickled Sweet-Sour Squash..69
Spiced Pickled Beets..70
Giardiniera 71
Sweet and Sour Pickled Zucchini Slices...............................72

CONCLUSION **73**

Recipe Index **74**

Conversion Tables **75**

Other Books by Kaitlyn Donnelly **76**

INTRODUCTION

People have been conserving food for centuries. With modern food technology, most people don't need it – you can pick up almost any type of product at a local grocery store. So, why worry about preserving your own food?

For me, it is a sense of pride. I grow my own fruits and, and it's nice that I can appreciate that produce all throughout the year.

Canning and preserving is not as hard as it looks. Understanding some basics will keep your food safe and keep you on the right track. Making your own preserves is a cinch once you get the hang of it.

CHAPTER 1. Canning Basics

Canning is a safe, important method for preserving food. The canning process involves placing products in jars or similar containers and heating them to a temperature that kills microorganisms that cause food spoilage. During this heating process, the air is expelled from the jar and, as it cools, a vacuum seal is made. This vacuum seal keeps food fresh and safe to eat later.

General Canning Methods

There are two ways of processing food, the pressure canner method and the boiling water bath method:

- The boiling water bath method is safe for fruits, tomatoes, jams, pickles, jellies, and other preserves. In this way, jars of food are completely heated in boiling water and cooked for a certain amount of time.

- The pressure canner method is safe for preserving meats, vegetables, seafood, and poultry. Jars of food are placed in a special pressure cooker in 2-3 inches of water that is heated to a temperature of at least 240°F.

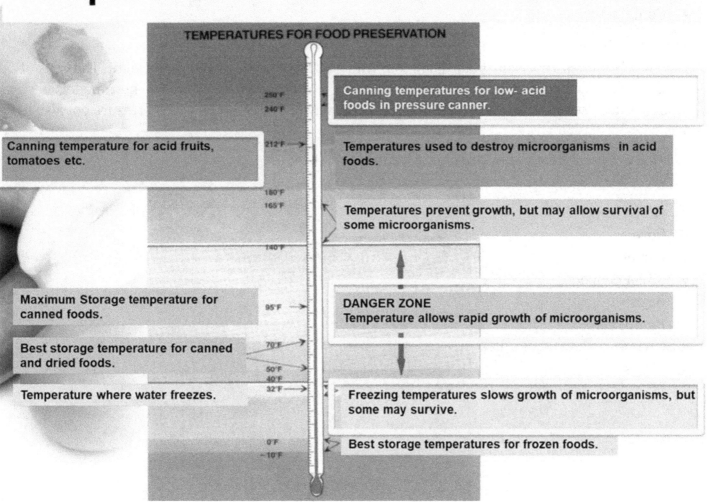

Temperatures for Food Preservation

Water Bath Canners

This method requires a large cooking pot, a tight-fitting lid, and a wooden or wire rack that keeps jars from touching each other. The rack lets the boiling water flow underneath and around the jars for more even sterilization. The rack also saves jars from bumping each other and breaking or cracking.

If you don't have a rack, you can use clean cotton dish towels to pack around the jars.

If you don't have a standard canner, use any large metal container as long as it is deep enough for 1-2 inches of fast boiling water to cover the jars.

Fruits and vegetables perfect for water bath canning include:

- Fruits
- Jams and jellies
- Fruit juices
- Fresh tomatoes (with added acid)
- Salsas
- Pickles and relishes
- Vinegar
- Chutneys
- Condiments

Pressure Canner

This method requires a specially made heavy pot with a lid that can be closed steam-tight. The lid is fitted with a safety fuse, a vent (or pet-cock), and a weighted or dial pressure gauge. The new models have an additional safety lock as an extra precaution. It may or may not have gaskets. The pressure pot also has a rack.

Foods that are perfect for pressure canning include:

- Potatoes
- Green beans
- Corn
- Carrots
- Sweet peppers
- Beets
- Pumpkins
- Greens
- Meats

Jars

Ball jars and Mason jars exactly designed for home canning are best. Do not use pickle jars, commercial mayonnaise jars, or baby food jars. Such jars are not made with heavy glass, the jars' mouths may be inappropriate for the sealing lids, and they cannot be heat treated.

Quart and pint Ball jars are the most frequently used sizes and are available in wide-mouth and regular tops. When properly used, jars may be used again and again indefinitely as long as they are in good condition.

Jar Lids

Most canning jars sold today use a self-sealing two-piece lid that consists of a separate screw-type metal band and a flat metal disc with a rubber-type sealing compound around one side near the outer edge. The flat lid is used only once but the screw band can be used over as long as it does not begin to rust and it is cleaned well.

Canning Utensils

Essential items for home canning and preserving:

- **Jar funnel:** helps in packing small food items and pouring liquid into canning jars.
- **Jar lifter:** necessary for easy removal of hot jars.
- **Lid wand:** a magnetized wand to remove treated jar lids from hot water.
- **Clean cloths:** handy for wiping jar rims, spills, and general cleaning.
- **Flat, narrow rubber spatula:** to remove trapped air bubbles before sealing jars.

Preparing Food

Always start with a reputable and proven recipe. There is a science behind the amounts of vinegar, sugar, or salt and the processing time of each recipe. None of the processing time or ingredient amounts should be changed unless the recipe says you can do this. Many tried and true recipes can be found in this beautiful canning book. These recipes have been used for generations.

- A proper recipe will provide the appropriate headspace amount and processing time. The headspace is the distance between the underside of the lid and the surface of food, which allows for bubbling up of liquid during processing or expansion of the food. The headspace is critical for proper sealing.
- Wash and sterilize your knife, cutting board, and any other equipment you ill use to prepare the recipe.
- Use unblemished, ripe products. This will not only give your finished product a delicious taste but will eliminate any bacteria living in the spoiled part of the vegetable or fruit and have the right color.
- Wash all products in warm water with a food-safe detergent. Your products can be contaminated with parasites, bacteria, and viruses anywhere from the garden to your table. This will protect your food from contamination before canning begins.

Store Home-Canned Foods Safely

Canned foods are versatile, easy, and long-lasting. But like many products, a lack of proper storage makes them landfills.

Here are three tips to keep your opened canned goods fresh:

1. **Use airtight containers**. Canned products can last a very long time, but only if they are sealed.
2. **Keep the liquid and brine**. After you have opened canned food, don't dispose of the brine or liquid.
3. **Store in the back of the refrigerator**. Keep resealed canned goods at the back of the fridge, where it is coldest. This also stops them from being subjected to temperature changes every time you open the fridge door.

It would be terribly shameful to spend so much energy and time canning jams, pickles, and veggies only to have spoil. Most homemade canned food can last up to a year in the pantry with proper storage.

To keep lovingly homemade canned foods from spoiling, it is important to keep them away from direct sun and store them in a dry, cool place. That does not mean that you have to keep your canned food in the refrigerator, but it does mean that they can be stored in the pantry to maximize their shelf life.

You will also want to remove the rings from your Mason jars when you store them. You need the ring while you are processing your canned foods, but once the canning is done, remove the ring. So, if the food spoils, your lid will pop up. Save those canning rings so you can use them to secure the lid if you do not use all of the jar's contents the first time. Once you have opened anything canned, you'll want to store it in the fridge and use it within a week of opening.

Good Things to Know about Syrup

Canned fruits often float if air remains in the fruit after processing, if the sugar syrup is too heavy, or if jars are packed too loosely. To avoid this, pack fruit tightly in jars without crushing, use a light or medium sugar syrup, and make sure fruit is ripe and firm.

It may darken during storage if fruit is not covered by liquid, but does not certainly mean it is spoiled. To avoid this, make sure fruit is covered with liquid while still leaving the recommended headspace. Also, remove trapped air bubbles with a kitchen knife, slim rubber scraper, or spatula. To do this efficiently, tilt the jar slightly by mooving the tool between the edge of the jar and the fruit and pressing inward against the fruit.

Canned apples, peaches, and pears may show a pink, blue, or red color change after processing. This is a natural chemical change that happen as fruits are heated.

A wooden spoon in the shape of a spatula that has a flat end instead of a round one, is good to have for mixing the sugar syrup in a flat bottom pan during the cooking process.

Avoid storing canned food near hot water pipes, a furnace, or water heater. Jars need to be kept cool to protect against spoilage and for longer storage life. Necessarily store in a dry place. Rusting of the band or lid can break the seal.

To prevent freezing in extremely cold storage environments, wrap the cans with newspaper and place in heavy cardboard boxes. If necessary, cover the boxes with a heavy cloth blanket.

Sugar Syrup

Syrup	Sugar	Water	Yield
Light	2 cups	4 cups	5 cups
Medium	3 cups	4 cups	5½ cups
Heavy	4 ¾ cups	4 cups	6½ cups

To prepare syrup: heat water and add sugar slowly, stirring constantly to dissolve. Bring to a gentle boil. Fill jars while the syrup is still boiling hot.

Frequently Asked Questions

When packing jars, is the headspace really important?

Yes, leaving the stated amount of headspace in a jar allows a vacuum seal during processing. If too little headspace, the food may expand and bubble out when air is being forced out from under the lid. The bubbling food can leave a deposit on the seal of the lid or the jar's rim and prevent the jar from sealing properly. If too much headspace, jars may not seal and the food at the top is likely to discolor.

How long can canned food be stored?

Properly preserved food stored in a dry, cool place will retain optimum eating quality for at least one year. Canned food stored in a warm place in indirect sunlight, near a furnace, hot pipes, or a range may lose some of its eating quality in a few weeks or months, depending on the temperature. Moisture can corrode metal lids or bands and cause leakage that will spoil the contents.

Do I need to sterilize the jars before processing?

There is no need to sterilize jars if they will be processed in a pressure canner or if they will be filled with food and processed in a boiling water bath canner for 10 minutes or more. However, it is worth using the extra time and sterilizing them anyway. When it comes to food safety, one can never be too careful.

Jars processed in a boiling water bath for less than 10 minutes should be sterilized by boiling them in hot water for 10 minutes before filling them.

Is it safe to use the oven for food processing?

No. This can be dangerous as the temperature will vary depending on the accuracy of the oven regulators and the heat circulation. Dry heat penetrates into jars of food very slowly. Jars can also easily explode in the oven.

Why do you need to exhaust a pressure canner?

If the pot is not exhausted, the temperature inside may not match the pressure on the gauge. Before closing the valve, the steam should be allowed to escape for 10 minutes.

Should liquid lost during processing be replaced?

No. Loss of liquid does not cause spoilage of the food, although food above the liquid may become darker.

Is it all right to reuse jar bands and lids?

Screw bands can be reused unless they are badly rusted or the top edge is pried up that would prevent a proper seal. Lids should never be reused since the sealing compound becomes indented by the first usage, preventing another airtight seal.

Is it safe to use the canning method of an open kettle?

No. This method means that food is cooked in a usual kettle (an open pot), then packed into hot jars and sealed without processing. The temperatures obtained are not hot enough to destroy all the dangerous microorganisms in the food. Contamination may also occur when transferring food from the kettle to the jars.

What causes the undersides of jar lids to discolor?

Natural compounds in some products, particularly acids, corrode metal and cause dark deposits on the underside of jar lids. This deposit is harmless providing the contents have been properly processed and the jar has a good seal.

Why do jars break down during processing?

Canning jars will break down for several reasons:

- Putting jars of unheated or raw food directly into boiling water in the canner. This rapid change of temperature is too high and will crack jars.
- Using commercial food jars
- Putting hot food in cold jars
- Using jars that have chips or cracks
- Jars bumping against each other during canning
- Placing jars directly on the bottom of canner instead of on a rack

Can hard water scale or film be removed from canning jars?

This can be often be accomplished by soaking jars for several hours in a solution of 1 gallon of water + 1 cup vinegar.

Questions About Canning Fruits and Vegetables

Is it safe to preserve food without salt?

Yes. Salt is only used for flavor and is not necessary to prevent spoilage.

Is it safe to preserve fruits without sugar?

Yes. Sugar is added to retain the shape of the fruit, improve flavor, and help stabilize color. It is not added as a preservative.

If aspirin is used, can vegetables and fruits be canned without heating?

No. Aspirin should not be used for preservation. It cannot be relied on to give satisfactory products or to prevent spoilage. Adequate heat treatment is the only safe procedure.

If vinegar is used, is it safe to can green beans in a boiling water bath?

No. Do not shorten recommended processing times if vinegar is used for preserving fresh vegetables (this does not refer to pickled vegetables).

Should I precook all vegetables before canning?

For best quality, yes. However, some vegetables can be packed cold or raw into jars before being processed in the pressure canner.

What vegetables expand rather than shrink during processing?

Lima beans, corn, and peas are starchy and expand during processing. They should be packed loosely.

What makes corn turn brown during canning?

Most often this occurs when too high a temperature is used, causing caramelization of the sugar in the corn. Also because of some minerals in the water used in canning.

Questions About Canning Meats

Is it safe to can poultry and meat without salt?

Yes. Salt is used only for flavoring and is not necessary for safe processing.

Should chicken giblets be canned in the same jar with chicken?

No. Their flavor may penetrate other pieces of chicken in the jar.

CHAPTER 2. Canning Fruit and Vegetables

Equipment Preparation

Wash and assemble canning utensils, containers, and equipment. Before you start preparing the fruit/vegetables, make sure you have everything you need. Once you start the canning process, you need to work as quickly as possible without delay.

Ball Canning Jars

Use authentic Ball or Mason canner jars. Examine and discard those with rough edges, nicks, and cracks. These defects will not allow the jar to hermetically seal. All jars need to be washed in hot water with soap, rinsed well and then kept hot to prevent breakage when they are filled with hot food and placed in the pot for processing.

Jars that are filled with food and processed for less than 10 minutes in a bath canner should be sterilized in boiling water for 10 minutes. NOTE: If you are at an altitude of 1000 feet or more, boil an additional minute for each additional 1000 feet of altitude (i.e., 6000 feet=6 minutes longer).

Fruit and Vegetable Preparation

Do not use over-ripe products. Purchase or collect only as much as you can prepare within 2-3 hours.

Wash the products with a quick soak and/or rinse, be sure to remove all sand and dirt, including any chemicals that may be present. Dirt contains some bacteria that are harder to kill. The cleaner the food, the more effective the preserving process. Do not use damaged or decayed fruit. Do not allow the food to soak, as it will lose nutrients and flavor.

Water Bath Canners

Fill the kettle with the hot water and begin heating it on the stove. The water bath requires 1-2 inches of water above the jars' tops. It may be difficult to determine how much water you need before the filled jars are in place, but after a batch or two you will find out how much water you need to add. It is good to have an extra small pot with hot water just in case.

Packing Jars

Raw Pack (Cold Pack)

Place raw fruit into jars and cover with boiling hot water or sugar syrup juice. It is necessary to leave a headspace between the top of food or liquid and the lid. This space is needed for fruit expansion and the bubbling of liquids. If the jars are too full, it may overflow during processing. The amount of headspace is usually between ⅛ and 1/2 inch. Pay attention to the individual recipe for the exact amount of headspace.

Hot Pack

Before packing, heat fruit in syrup, water, or steam. Tomatoes and fruits with a high juice content can be preheated without adding liquid and then packed in the juice that cooks out.

To Fill Jars

Pack each jar to within ¼ inch of top or as directed in the recipe. For non-liquid foods (i.e., peaches) it is essential to remove any air bubbles by running a table knife or rubber spatula gently between the edge of the jar and the solid product. If necessary, add more hot syrup. Wipe rim and screw threads with a damp cloth, place lid on top and screw bands on firmly and evenly to hold rubber sealing lid in place. Sometimes you may need to hold down the sealing lid while you tighten the band to make sure the lid is centered on the jar's top. Do not over-tighten. The jars are now ready to be placed on the rack inside the hot water canner.

General Processing

Water Bath Method

After packing, immediately place jars on the rack. Lower filled rack into canner. Jars have to be covered by 1-2 inches of water. If needed, add additional boiling water. When adding more water, pour between jars and not directly on them. Cover the pot with a lid. Start the processing time when the water comes to a rolling boil. Boil steadily for the time that is recommended for the food being processed. Remove jars when the cooking time is up and place on a rack or on towels away from any draft and away from heat.

Test for Seal

Check seal after jars have cooled, 12-24 hours after processing. To do this, press down on the lid center. The lid should be not concave when pressed. Another method is to knock the lid with the bottom of a teaspoon. It will make a high-pitched sound if the jar is sealed correctly. If it produces a dull sound, it means the lid is not sealed perfectly or food is in contact with the lid underside. Don't worry if you hear a popping sound coming out of the jar for the first hour or so before getting cold. This is a good sound as it most often means that the vacuum effect has taken place, which causes the lids to seal and pop down.

If desired, the screw bands may be removed after jars have cooled thoroughly. Label canned jars with processing date and contents. Store jars in a dry, cool, dark place.

Canning Tomatoes

Traditionally, tomatoes are usually canned by using the hot water bath canner method. Lately, however, more people are discovering that canning tomatoes in a pressure canner will give you a more nutritious product and result in higher quality.

Pressure canning is also needed for many canned tomato combination products since the pH value is above 4.6. The tomatoes themselves fall close to the low acid level, just slightly above 4.6, and when mixed with vegetables like peppers or zucchini or with meat for sauces, it increases the pH value above 4.6 and has to be processed by pressure canning to ensure food safety. Foods with a pH value of 4.6 or lower can be processed in a boiling water bath canner.

When canning tomatoes, it is recommended that you add acid to lower the pH level. You can do this by adding ¼ teaspoon citric acid or 1 tablespoon of lemon juice per pint of product. For quarts, add ½ teaspoon citric acid or 2 tablespoons of lemon juice. You can do this by adding directly to jars before filling.

Skinning tomatoes

With a knife, cut an X on the bottom of the tomatoes before putting in a pot of boiling water for 30-60 seconds. Fish out with a slotted spoon, plunge into a bowl of cold water (or an ice bath), lift them directly back out, and peel the skin with a knife or fingers. It will slip off like a charm.

Preparing jams, butters, marmalades, and jellies

- Sweet spreads consist of fruits conserved mostly by means of sugar and they are jellied or thickened to some extent.
- Fruit jelly is a semi-solid mixture of sugar and fruit juice that is clear and firm enough to hold its shape.
- Preserves are made of whole, small fruits or uniform-size pieces of fruit in a slightly thick, clear, jellied syrup.
- Jam will also hold its shape, but it is less firm than jelly. Jam is made from sugar and chopped or crushed fruits. Jams made from a fruit mixture are usually called conserves, especially when they include nuts, citrus fruits, raisins, or coconut.
- Fruit butter is made from fruit pulp and cooked with sugar until thickened to a spreadable consistency.
- Marmalades are soft fruit jellies with small pieces of citrus or fruit peel evenly suspended in a transparent jelly.

For the right consistency, jellied fruit products need the correct combination of sugar, fruit, pectin, and acid. Flavorful, good-quality fruits make the best-jellied products.

Sugar serves as a preservative, aids in gelling, and contributes flavor. Beet and cane sugar are the usual sources of sugar for jam or jelly. Honey and corn syrup may be used to replace part of the sugar in recipes, but too much will alter the structure and mask the fruit flavor. Use tested recipes for replacing sugar with corn syrup and honey. Do not reduce the amount of sugar in traditional recipes. Too little sugar may allow molds and yeasts to grow and prevents gelling.

CHAPTER 3. Recipes
JAM and JELLY

Apricot Amaretto Jam

Prep time: 30 minutes

Cooking time: 10 minutes

Yield: 8 half-pints

Nutrients per 2 tablespoons:

Carbohydrates – 21 g

Fat – 0 g

Protein – 0 g

Calories – 86

Ingredients:

- 4¼ cups peeled, crushed apricots
- ¼ cup lemon juice
- 6¼ cups sugar, divided
- 1 package powdered fruit pectin
- ½ teaspoon unsalted butter
- ⅓ cup amaretto

Instructions:

1. In a Dutch oven, combine lemon juice and apricots.
2. In a small bowl, combine pectin and ¼ cup sugar. Stir into apricot mixture and add butter. Bring to a full boil over medium-high heat, stirring constantly.
3. Stir in the remaining sugar and let boil 1-2 minutes, stirring constantly.

4. Remove from heat and stir in amaretto.
5. Let the jam sit for 5 minutes, stirring occasionally.
6. Divide the hot mixture between eight hot sterilized half-pint jars, leaving ¼-inch space of the top. Wipe the rims carefully. Place tops on jars and screw on bands until fingertip tight.
7. Place jars into canner with boiling water, ensuring that they are completely covered with water. Let boil for 10 minutes. Remove jars and cool.

Raspberry Peach Jam

Prep time: 35 minutes

Cooking time: 15 minutes

Yield: 3 half-pints

Nutrients per 2 tablespoons:

Carbohydrates – 8 g

Fat – 0 g

Protein – 0 g

Calories – 33

Ingredients:

- 2⅔ cups peeled, chopped peaches
- 1½ cups crushed raspberries
- 3 cups sugar
- 1½ tsp lemon juice

Instructions:

1. In a Dutch oven, combine all ingredients.
2. Cook over medium-low heat. Stir until the sugar has dissolved and the mixture is bubbly, about 10 minutes.
3. Bring to a full boil for 15 minutes, stirring constantly.
4. Remove from heat and skim off foam.
5. Carefully scoop the hot mixture into hot sterilized half-pint jars, leaving ¼-inch space of the top. Remove air bubbles. Wipe the rims carefully. Place tops on jars and screw on bands until fingertip tight.
6. Place jars into canner with boiling water, ensuring that they are completely covered with water. Let boil for 15 minutes. Remove jars and cool

Blueberry Cinnamon Jam

Prep time: 35 minutes

Cooking time: 10 minutes per batch

Yield: 9 half-pints

Nutrients per 2 tablespoons:

Carbohydrates – 19 g

Fat – 0 g

Protein – 0 g

Calories – 74

Ingredients:

- 8 cups fresh blueberries
- 6 cups sugar
- 3 tbsp lemon juice
- 2 tsp ground cinnamon
- 2 tsp grated lemon zest
- ½ tsp ground nutmeg
- 2 (3 oz) pouches liquid fruit pectin

Instructions:

1. Place blueberries in a food processor and process until well blended. Transfer to a stockpot.
2. Stir in the lemon juice, sugar, cinnamon, nutmeg, and lemon zest. Bring to a rolling boil over high heat, stirring constantly.
3. Stir in pectin. Boil for 1 minute, stirring constantly.
4. Remove from the heat; skim off foam.
5. Scoop the hot mixture in hot sterilized half-pint jars, leaving ¼-inch space of the top. Remove air bubbles. Wipe the rims carefully. Place tops on jars and screw on bands until fingertip tight.
6. Place jars into canner with boiling water, ensuring that they are completely covered with water. Let boil for 10 minutes. Remove jars and cool.

Carrot Pineapple Pear Jam

Prep time: 45 minutes

Cooking time: 5 minutes

Yield: 8 half-pints

Nutrients per 2 tablespoons:

Carbohydrates – 23 g

Fat – 0 g

Protein – 0 g

Sodium – 2 mg

Calories – 88

Ingredients:

- 20 oz crushed pineapple, undrained
- 1½ cups peeled, shredded carrots
- 1½ cups ripe, peeled, chopped pears
- 3 tbsp lemon juice
- 1 tsp ground cinnamon
- ¼ tsp ground cloves
- ¼ tsp ground nutmeg
- 1 package powdered fruit pectin
- 6½ cups sugar

Instructions:

1. In a saucepan over medium heat, combine first 7 ingredients and bring to a boil.
2. Reduce heat and simmer, covered, until pears are tender, 15-20 minutes, stirring occasionally.
3. Add pectin. Bring to a full boil, stirring constantly.
4. Stir in sugar. Boil and stir for 1 minute.
5. Remove from heat and skim off foam.
6. Scoop the hot mixture in hot sterilized half-pint jars, leaving ¼-inch space of the top. Remove air bubbles and if necessary, adjust headspace by adding hot mixture. Wipe the rims carefully. Place tops on jars and screw on bands until fingertip tight.
7. Place jars into canner with boiling water, ensuring that they are completely covered with water. Let boil for 10 minutes. Remove jars and cool.

Green Tomato Jam

Prep time: 10 minutes

Cooking time: 20 minutes

Yield: 3 half-pints

Nutrients per 2 tablespoons:

Carbohydrates – 20 g

Fat – 0 g

Protein – 1 g

Sodium – 10 mg

Calories – 81

Ingredients:

- 2½ cups pureed green tomatoes
- 2 cups sugar
- 1 package raspberry gelatin

Instructions:

1. In a large saucepan, bring sugar and tomatoes to a boil.
2. Reduce heat and let simmer, uncovered, for 20 minutes.
3. Remove from the heat and add gelatin, stirring until dissolved.
4. Skim off any foam.
5. Scoop the hot mixture in hot sterilized half-pint jars, leaving ¼-inch space of the top. Remove air bubbles and if necessary, adjust headspace by adding hot mixture. Wipe the rims carefully. Let cool before covering with lids. Refrigerate up to 3 weeks.

Pineapple Rhubarb Jam

Prep time: 15 minutes

Cooking time: 30 minutes

Yield: 7 half-pints

Nutrients per 2 tablespoons:

Carbohydrates – 23 g

Fat – 0 g

Protein – 0 g

Sodium – 7 mg

Calories – 89

Ingredients:

- 5 cups sliced fresh rhubarb
- 5 cups sugar
- 1 (20 oz) can unsweetened crushed pineapple, undrained
- ¼ cup water
- 1 (6 oz) package strawberry gelatin

Instructions:

1. In a Dutch oven, combine pineapple, rhubarb, sugar, and water. Bring to a boil.
2. Reduce heat and simmer, uncovered, for 20 minutes or until rhubarb is broken down, stirring occasionally.
3. Add gelatin and stir until dissolved.
4. Remove from heat and skim off foam.
5. Scoop the hot mixture in hot sterilized half-pint jars, leaving ¼-inch space of the top. Remove air bubbles and if necessary, adjust headspace by adding hot mixture. Wipe the rims carefully. Place tops on jars and screw on bands until fingertip tight.
6. Place jars into canner with boiling water, ensuring that they are completely covered with water. Let boil for 10 minutes. Remove jars and cool.

Plum Orange Jam

Prep time: 30 minutes

Cooking time: 5 minutes

Yield: 10 half-pints

Nutrients per 2 tablespoons:

Carbohydrates – 13 g

Fat – 0 g

Protein – 0 g

Calories – 50

Ingredients:

- 10 cups chopped plums, skinless
- 1 cup orange juice
- 1 package pectin
- 3 cups sugar
- 3 tbsp grated orange zest
- 1½ tsp ground cinnamon

Instructions:

1. In a Dutch oven, combine orange juice and plums and bring to a boil.
2. Reduce heat and simmer, covered, 5-7 minutes or until softened, stirring occasionally.
3. Stir in pectin. Bring to a rolling boil, stirring constantly.
4. Stir in cinnamon, sugar, and orange zest. Let boil for 1 minute, stirring until sugar completely dissolves.

5. Remove from heat and skim off foam.
6. Scoop the hot mixture in hot sterilized half-pint jars, leaving ¼-inch space of the top. Remove air bubbles and if necessary, adjust headspace by adding hot mixture. Wipe the rims carefully. Place tops on jars and screw on bands until fingertip tight.
7. Place jars into canner with boiling water, ensuring that they are completely covered with water. Let boil for 5 minutes. Remove jars and cool.

Ginger Pear Freezer Jam

Prep time: 30 minutes (+24 hours)

Cooking time: 10 minutes

Yield: 7 cups

Nutrients per 2 tablespoons:

Carbohydrates – 17 g

Fat – 0 g

Protein – 0 g

Sodium – 9 mg

Calories – 64

Ingredients:

- 5½ cups fresh, peeled, chopped pears
- 1 package pectin
- 2 tbsp lemon juice
- 1½ tsp grated lemon zest
- 1 tsp fresh, minced ginger root
- 4 cups sugar
- 1 tsp vanilla extract

Instructions:

1. In a Dutch oven, combine pears, lemon juice, pectin, lemon zest, and ginger. Bring to a rolling boil, stirring constantly.
2. Stir in sugar. Let boil for 1 minute, stirring constantly. Stir in vanilla.
3. Remove from heat and skim off foam.
4. Scoop the hot mixture in hot sterilized 1-cup containers, leaving ¼-inch space of the top. Remove air bubbles and if necessary, adjust headspace by adding hot mixture. Wipe the rims carefully. Place tops on.
5. Allow jam to set for about 24 hours.

Pina Colada Zucchini Jam

Prep time: 15 minutes

Cooking time: 20 minutes

Yield: 7 half-pints

Nutrients per 2 tablespoons:

Carbohydrates – 25 g

Fat – 0 g

Protein – 0 g

Sodium – 8 mg

Calories – 100

Ingredients:

- 6 cups peeled, shredded zucchini
- 1 (8oz) can crushed pineapple, undrained
- 6 cups sugar
- ¼ cup lime juice
- 2 (3 oz) packages pineapple gelatin
- 1 tsp rum extract

Instructions:

1. In a Dutch oven, combine zucchini, pineapple, lime juice, and sugar. Bring to a boil and cook for 10 minutes, stirring constantly.
2. Remove from heat and stir in rum extract and gelatin until gelatin is dissolved.
3. Remove from heat and skim off foam.
4. Scoop the hot mixture in hot sterilized half-pint jars, leaving ¼-inch space of the top. Remove air bubbles and if necessary, adjust headspace by adding hot mixture. Wipe the rims carefully. Place tops on jars and screw on bands until fingertip tight.
5. Place jars into canner with boiling water, ensuring that they are completely covered with water. Let boil for 10 minutes. Remove jars and cool.

Strawberry Freezer Jam

Prep time: 30 minutes (+24 hours)

Cooking time: 10 minutes

Yield: 4½ pints

Nutrients per 2 tablespoons:

Carbohydrates – 20 g

Fat – 0 g

Protein – 0 g

Sodium – 3 mg

Calories – 79

Ingredients:

- 4 cups fresh, washed, mashed strawberries
- 5½ cups sugar
- 1 cup light corn syrup
- ¼ cup lemon juice
- ¾ cup water
- 1 package powdered fruit pectin

Instructions:

1. Place strawberries in a large bowl. Add lemon juice, sugar, and corn syrup. Let stand 10 minutes.

2. In a Dutch oven, combine strawberry mixture, pectin, and water. Bring to a rolling boil and boil for 1 minute, stirring constantly.

3. Remove from heat and skim off foam.

4. Pour into freezer containers or sterilized jars, leaving ¼-inch space of the top. Cover and let stand about 24 hours. Refrigerate up to 3 weeks or freeze containers up to 12 months. Defrost frozen jam in the refrigerator before serving.

Caramel Apple Jam

Prep time: 30 minutes

Cooking time: 10 minutes

Yield: 7 half-pints

Nutrients per 2 tablespoons:

Carbohydrates – 21 g

Fat – 0 g

Protein – 0 g

Sodium – 4 mg

Calories – 83

Ingredients:

- 6 cups fresh, peeled, diced apples
- ½ cup water
- ½ tsp butter
- ½ tsp ground cinnamon
- ¼ tsp ground nutmeg
- 1 package powdered fruit pectin
- 3 cups sugar
- 2 cups brown sugar

Instructions:

1. In a Dutch oven, combine the apples, butter, water, nutmeg, and cinnamon. Cook, stirring, over low heat until apples are tender.
2. Stir in pectin. Bring to a boil.
3. Stir in sugar and let boil, stirring, for 1 minute.
4. Remove from heat and skim off foam.
5. Scoop the hot mixture in hot sterilized half-pint jars, leaving ¼-inch space of the top. Remove air bubbles and if necessary, adjust headspace by adding hot mixture. Wipe the rims carefully. Place tops on jars and screw on bands until fingertip tight
6. Place jars into canner with boiling water, ensuring that they are completely covered with water. Let boil for 10 minutes. Remove jars and cool.

Christmas Cranberry Jam

Prep time: 25 minutes

Cooking time: 10 minutes

Yield: 14 half-pints

Nutrients per 2 tablespoons:

Carbohydrates – 22 g

Fat – 0 g

Protein – 0 g

Calories – 84

Ingredients:

- 2½ lbs frozen unsweetened strawberries, thawed or fresh strawberries, hulled
- 1 lb fresh or frozen cranberries, thawed
- 5 lbs sugar
- 2 (3 oz) pouches liquid fruit pectin

Instructions:

1. Blend cranberries and strawberries in a food processor until smooth, then pour into a Dutch oven.
2. Add sugar and bring to a boil. Let boil for 1 minute.
3. Stir in pectin and return to a boil. Boil for 1 minute, stirring constantly.
4. Cool for 5 minutes and skim off foam.
5. Scoop the hot mixture in hot sterilized half-pint jars, leaving ¼-inch space of the top. Remove air bubbles and if necessary, adjust headspace by adding hot mixture. Wipe the rims carefully. Place tops on jars and screw on bands until fingertip tight
6. Place jars into canner with boiling water, ensuring that they are completely covered with water. Let boil for 10 minutes. Remove jars and cool.

Candy Apple Jelly

Prep time: 10 minutes

Cooking time: 5 minutes

Yield: 6 half-pints

Nutrients per 2 tablespoons:

Carbohydrates – 24 g

Fat – 0 g

Protein – 0 g

Sodium – 1 mg

Calories – 92

Ingredients:

- 4 cups apple juice
- ½ cup Red Hots candy
- 1 package powdered fruit pectin
- 4½ cups sugar

Instructions:

1. In a large saucepan, combine the candies, apple juice, and pectin. Bring to a rolling boil, stirring constantly.
2. Stir in sugar and let boil, stirring, for 1 minute.
3. Remove from heat and skim off foam.
4. Scoop the hot mixture in hot sterilized half-pint jars, leaving ¼-inch space of the top. Remove air bubbles and if necessary, adjust headspace by adding hot mixture. Wipe the rims carefully. Place tops on jars and screw on bands until fingertip tight.
5. Place jars into canner with boiling water, ensuring that they are completely covered with water. Let boil for 5 minutes. Remove jars and cool.

Lime Mint Jelly

Prep time: 10 minutes

Cooking time: 10 minutes

Yield: 5 half-pints

Nutrients per 2 tablespoons:

Carbohydrates – 21 g

Fat – 0 g

Protein – 0 g

Sodium – 1 mg

Calories – 79

Ingredients:

- 4 cups sugar
- 1¾ cups water
- ¾ cup lime juice
- 3 drops green food coloring
- 1 (3 oz) package liquid fruit pectin
- 3 tbsp chopped fresh mint leaves
- ¼ cup grated lime zest

Instructions:

1. In a large saucepan, combine lime juice, sugar, water, and food coloring. Bring to a rolling boil, stirring constantly.
2. Stir in lime zest pectin, and mint. Continue boiling for 1 minute, stirring constantly.
3. Remove from heat and skim off foam.
4. Scoop the hot mixture in hot sterilized half-pint jars, leaving ¼-inch space of the top. Remove air bubbles and if necessary, adjust headspace by adding hot mixture. Wipe the rims carefully. Place tops on jars and screw on bands until fingertip tight.
5. Place jars into canner with boiling water, ensuring that they are completely covered with water. Let boil for 10 minutes. Remove jars and cool.

Watermelon Jelly

Prep time: 25 minutes

Cooking time: 10 minutes

Yield: 5 half-pints

Nutrients per 2 tablespoons:

Carbohydrates – 27 g

Fat – 0 g

Protein – 0 g

Sodium – 1 mg

Calories – 106

Ingredients:

- 6 cups chopped, seeded watermelon
- ⅓ cup white wine vinegar
- 5 cups sugar
- ¼ cup lemon juice
- 2 drops red food coloring
- 2 (3 oz) pouches liquid fruit pectin

Instructions:

1. Blend watermelon in a food processor until pureed. Place pureed watermelon in a cheesecloth-lined strainer, with a bowl underneath to capture liquid. Let stand 10 minutes until liquid measures 2 cups.
2. Discard watermelon pulp from cheesecloth, and place the liquid in a large saucepan.
3. Stir in vinegar, sugar, lemon juice, and food coloring. Bring to a boil, stirring constantly.
4. Stir in pectin. Continue boiling for 1 minute, stirring constantly.
5. Remove from heat and skim off foam.
6. Scoop the hot mixture in hot sterilized half-pint jars, leaving ¼-inch space of the top. Remove air bubbles and if necessary, adjust headspace by adding hot mixture. Wipe the rims carefully. Place tops on jars and screw on bands until fingertip tight
7. Place jars into canner with boiling water, ensuring that they are completely covered with water. Let boil for 10 minutes. Remove jars and cool.

Cucumber Jelly

Prep time: 15 minutes

Cooking time: 10 minutes

Yield: 8 half-pints

Nutrients per 2 tablespoons:

Carbohydrates – 25 g

Fat – 0 g

Protein – 0 g

Sodium – 1 mg

Calories – 35

Ingredients:

- 2½ cups cucumber juice, strained
- 7 cups sugar
- 1 cup vinegar
- Seeds scraped from one vanilla bean.
- 2 pouches pectin

Instructions:

1. Mix first four ingredients in a pot and bring to a boil, stirring occasionally. Let boil for 2 minutes, then remove from heat.
2. Stir in the pectin, then return to a boil. Boil and stir for 1-2 minutes.
3. Remove from heat and skim off foam.
4. Scoop jelly into hot sterilized half-pint jars, leaving ¼ inch headspace. Remove air bubbles and if necessary, adjust

headspace by adding hot mixture. Wipe the rims carefully. Place tops on jars and screw on bands until fingertip tight.
5. Place jars into canner with boiling water, ensuring that they are completely covered with water. Let boil for 10 minutes. Remove jars and cool.

SWEET TREATS

Plum Cranberry Walnut Conserve

Prep time: 40 minutes

Cooking time: 10 minutes

Yield: 7 half-pints

Nutrients per 2 tablespoons:

Carbohydrates – 18 g

Fat – 0 g

Protein – 2 g

Calories – 81

Ingredients:

- 2 lbs medium Italian plums, skin on, pitted, quartered
- 1½ cups dried cranberries
- ½ cup quartered, thinly sliced mandarin oranges
- 1 cup coarsely chopped walnuts
- ½ cup orange juice
- 3 cups sugar
- 1 package powdered fruit pectin

Instructions:

1. In a Dutch oven, combine plums, oranges, cranberries, orange juice, and 2½ cups sugar. Mix the remaining sugar with pectin and set aside. Bring to a rolling boil over high heat, stirring, until slightly thickened and plums soften, about 15 minutes.

2. Stir in walnuts and pectin mixture and return let boil, stirring, for 1 minute.

3. Remove from heat and skim off foam.

4. Scoop the hot mixture in hot sterilized half-pint jars, leaving ¼-inch space of the top. Remove air bubbles and if necessary, adjust headspace by adding hot mixture. Wipe the rims carefully. Place tops on jars and screw on bands until fingertip tight.

5. Place jars into canner with boiling water, ensuring that they are completely covered with water. Let boil for 10 minutes. Remove jars and cool.

Glazed Carrots

Prep time: 15 minutes

Cooking time: 30 minutes

Yield: 16 pints

Nutrients per ¼ cup:

Carbohydrates – 3 g

Fat – 0 g

Protein – 0 g

Sodium – 87 mg

Calories – 12

Ingredients:

- 10 lbs carrots, washed, peeled, cut into 2-inch pieces
- 8 cups brown sugar
- 8 cups water
- 4 cups orange juice

Instructions:

1. Pack carrots into hot sterilized pint jars, leaving 1-inch of the top.
2. In a saucepan over medium heat, mix the orange juice, brown sugar, and water. Stir until sugar is dissolved.
3. Scoop hot mixture over carrots, leaving ¼ inch headspace. Remove air bubbles and if necessary, adjust headspace by adding hot mixture. Wipe the rims carefully. Place tops on jars and screw on bands until fingertip tight.
4. Place jars into canner with boiling water, ensuring that they are completely covered with water. Let boil for 30 minutes. Remove jars and cool.

Lemon Marmalade

Prep time: 40 minutes

Cooking time: 10 minutes

Yield: 6 half-pints

Nutrients per 2 tablespoons:

Carbohydrates – 17 g

Fat – 0 g

Protein – 0 g

Sodium – 0 mg

Calories – 67

Ingredients

- 3 medium lemons
- 1 medium grapefruit
- 4 cups water
- 1 (1¾ oz)package powdered fruit pectin
- 4 cups sugar

Instructions:

1. Peel rind from lemons and grapefruit, then cut into 1-inch long strips.
2. In a Dutch oven, combine citrus peel and water. Bring to a boil. Reduce heat and simmer, covered, 5-7 minutes, until peel is softened. Remove from heat and set aside.
3. Trim white pith from reserved grapefruit and lemons. Cut grapefruit and lemons into segments, discarding seeds and membranes.
4. Chop pulp, reserving juices, and stir into reserved peel mixture.
5. Add pectin. Bring to a boil, stirring constantly.
6. Stir in sugar and let boil, stirring, 1 minute.
7. Remove from heat and skim off foam.
8. Scoop hot mixture into six hot sterilized half-pint jars, leaving ¼-inch headspace. Remove air bubbles and if necessary, adjust headspace by adding hot mixture. Wipe the rims carefully. Place tops on jars and screw on bands until fingertip tight.
9. Place jars into canner with boiling water, ensuring that they are completely covered with water. Let boil for 10 minutes. Remove jars and cool.

Raisin Pear Chutney

Prep time: 2 hours 15 minutes

Cooking time: 15 minutes

Yield: 2 pints

Nutrients per ¼ cup:

Carbohydrates – 40 g

Fat – 0 g

Protein – 1 g

Sodium – 9 mg

Calories – 152

Ingredients:

- 2 cups cider vinegar
- 1¼ cups packed brown sugar
- 3 lbs unpeeled ripe pears, diced
- 1 medium onion, chopped
- 1 cup raisins
- 2 tsp ground cinnamon
- 1 tsp ground cloves
- 1 garlic clove, minced
- ½-1 tsp cayenne pepper

Instructions:

1. In a saucepan, bring brown sugar and vinegar to a boil.
2. Stir in the remaining ingredients and return to a boil.
3. Reduce heat and let simmer, uncovered, for 2 hours to 2 hours 15 minutes until chutney reaches desired consistency.

4. Carefully scoop hot mixture into hot sterilized pint jars, leaving ¼-inch headspace. Remove air bubbles and if necessary, adjust headspace by adding hot mixture. Wipe the rims carefully. Place tops on jars and screw on bands until fingertip tight.
5. Place jars into canner with boiling water, ensuring that they are completely covered with water. Let boil for 15 minutes. Remove jars and cool.

Chunky Peach Spread

Prep time: 20 minutes

Cooking time: 10 minutes

Yield: 3½ cups

Nutrients per 2 tablespoons:

Carbohydrates – 6 g

Fat – 0 g

Protein – 1 g

Sodium – 1 mg

Calories – 25

Ingredients:

- 2½ lbs peaches, peeled, chopped
- 1 tbsp lemon juice
- 1 envelope unflavored gelatin
- ¼ cup cold water
- ⅓ cup sugar

Instructions:

1. In a bowl, mix gelatin and cold water.
2. In a saucepan, combine peaches, lemon juice, and sugar; bring to a boil. Mash peaches.
3. Reduce heat and let simmer, uncovered, 5 minutes.
4. Add gelatin mixture and cook 1 minute, stirring until gelatin is completely dissolved.
5. Cool 10 minutes.
6. Pour into sterilized jars. Refrigerate, covered, up to 3 weeks.

Apple-Walnut Maple Confiture

Prep time: 55 minutes

Cooking time: 10 minutes

Yield: 11 half-pints

Nutrients per 2 tablespoons:

Carbohydrates – 19 g

Fat – 2 g

Protein – 0 g

Sodium – 2 mg

Calories – 89

Ingredients:

- 12 cups peeled chopped Granny Smith apples
- 4 cups sugar
- 2 cups packed brown sugar
- 1 cup maple syrup
- 1 tsp pumpkin pie spice
- 1 tsp ground cinnamon
- 2 cups finely chopped walnuts, toasted

Instructions:

1. In a stockpot, combine first six ingredients and bring to a boil. Cook, uncovered, 20-30 minutes until mixture is slightly thickened and apples are tender.
2. Stir in walnuts. Return to a boil and cook, stirring, another 5 minutes longer.
3. Carefully scoop hot mixture into hot sterilized half-pint jars, leaving ¼-inch headspace. Remove air bubbles and if necessary, adjust headspace by adding hot mixture. Wipe the rims carefully. Place tops on jars and screw on bands until fingertip tight.
4. Place jars into canner with boiling water, ensuring that they are completely covered with water. Let boil; for 10 minutes. Remove jars and cool.

Spicy Roasted Beet Marmalade

Prep time: 1 hour 30 minutes

Cooking time: 1 hour

Yield: 2 half-pints

Nutrients per 2 tablespoons:

Carbohydrates – 32 g

Fat – 0 g

Protein – 1 g

Sodium – 63 mg

Calories – 132

Ingredients:

- 2½ lbs fresh beets
- 1 tbsp canola oil
- 1 medium lemon, peeled, thinly sliced, seedless
- 1 cup sugar
- 1 cup packed brown sugar
- ⅓ cup maple syrup
- 2 tbsp finely chopped crystallized ginger
- ⅛ teaspoon salt
- 1 cinnamon stick
- 8 whole cloves

Instructions:

1. Preheat oven to 400°F.
2. Peel beets and cut into wedges. Place in a baking pan; drizzle with canola oil and toss to coat. Roast 50-60 minutes or until tender. Cool slightly.
3. Rinse two 1-cup plastic containers and lids with boiling water. Dry thoroughly.

4. Tie cinnamon stick and cloves in a cheesecloth.
5. Process beets in a food processor until finely chopped. Transfer to a saucepan.
6. Add sugars, sliced lemon, maple syrup, ginger, salt, and spice bag. Bring to a boil, then simmer, uncovered, 1 to 1 hour 15 minutes until thickened.
7. Remove from heat, discard spice bag, and let cool slightly.
8. Fill 1-cup containers to within ½ inch of tops. Cover with lids. Refrigerate up to 7 days or freeze up to 12 months. Thaw frozen jam in refrigerator before serving.

Spiced Cran-Apple and Grape Confiture

Prep time: 2 hours

Cooking time: 5 minutes

Yield: 10 half-pints

Nutrients per 2 tablespoons:

Carbohydrates – 20 g

Fat – 0 g

Protein – 0 g

Sodium – 2 mg

Calories – 77

Ingredients:

- 4 cups peeled chopped tart apples
- 8 cups seedless red grapes
- 4 cups coarsely chopped fresh cranberries
- 6 cups sugar
- 3 tbsp lemon juice + enough water to equal 1 cup
- 1½ tsp ground cinnamon
- 1 cup peeled shredded tart apple
- 6 whole cloves
- 6 whole allspice berries

Instructions:

1. Tie cloves and allspice berries in a cheesecloth bag.
2. In a stockpot, combine first six ingredients and spice bag. Bring to a boil. Reduce heat and simmer about 45 minutes, uncovered, until mixture begins to thicken.

3. Add shredded apple and simmer until thickened, 35-45 minutes longer.
4. Discard spice bag.
5. Carefully scoop hot mixture into hot sterilized half-pint jars, leaving ¼-inch headspace. Remove air bubbles and if necessary, adjust headspace by adding hot mixture. Wipe the rims carefully. Place tops on jars and screw on bands until fingertip tight.
6. Place jars into canner with boiling water, ensuring that they are completely covered with water. Let boil; for 5 minutes. Remove jars and cool.

Rhubarb Cherry Chutney

Prep time: 20 minutes

Cooking time: 35 minutes

Yield: 6 cups

Nutrients per 2 tablespoons:

Carbohydrates – 27 g

Fat – 0 g

Protein – 0 g

Sodium – 3 mg

Calories – 102

Ingredients:

- 2 lbs chopped fresh rhubarb
- 2 cups fresh pitted tart cherries, chopped
- 1 large tart apple, peeled, chopped
- 1 medium red onion, chopped
- 1 celery rib, chopped
- 3 garlic cloves, minced
- 1 tbsp finely chopped crystallized ginger
- 2 cups brown sugar
- 1 cup red wine vinegar
- ¾ tsp ground cinnamon
- ½ tsp ground coriander
- ¼ tsp ground cloves

Instructions:

1. In a 6-quart stockpot, combine all ingredients. Bring to a boil.

2. Reduce heat and simmer, uncovered, 25-30 minutes, until thickened.

3. Transfer to covered containers. If freezing, use freezer-safe containers and fill to within ½ inch of tops. Freeze up to 12 months or refrigerate up to 3 weeks. Before serving thaw frozen salsa in the refrigerator.

Tomato Lemon Confiture

Prep time: 75 minutes

Cooking time: 10 minutes

Yield: 9 half-pints

Nutrients per 2 tablespoons:

Carbohydrates – 36 g

Fat – 0 g

Protein – 0 g

Sodium – 3 mg

Calories – 142

Ingredients:

- 5 medium ripe tomatoes
- 4 cups chopped peeled tart apples
- 2 medium lemons, seeded, finely chopped
- 8 whole cloves
- 2¼ tsp ground ginger
- 6 cups sugar

Instructions:

1. Peel, quarter, remove seeds and chop the tomatoes, then place in a colander to drain.
2. In a Dutch oven, combine the tomatoes, lemons, and apples. Cook, stirring, over medium heat for 15 minutes.
3. Add ginger and sugar.
4. Tie cloves in a cheesecloth and add to the pot.

5. Bring to a boil. Stir until sugar has dissolved. Reduce heat and simmer for 40 minutes, stirring frequently.
6. Remove spice bag. Carefully scoop hot mixture into nine hot sterilized half-pint jars, leaving ¼-inch headspace. Remove air bubbles and if necessary, adjust headspace by adding hot mixture. Wipe the rims carefully. Place tops on jars and screw on bands until fingertip tight.
7. Place jars into canner with boiling water, ensuring that they are completely covered with water. Let boil for 10 minutes. Remove jars and cool.

TOMATO TREATS

Canned Zucchini Salad

Prep time: 40 minutes

Cooking time: 20 minutes

Yield: 10 cups

Nutrients per 2 tablespoons:

Carbohydrates – 2 g

Protein – 0 g

Sodium – 45 mg

Calories – 20

Ingredients:

- 6 cups zucchini, diced into ½-inch cubes
- 7½ cups tomatoes, sliced
- 4 big bell peppers, sliced
- 4-5 garlic cloves, minced
- ¼ cup honey
- 1 tbsp salt
- 1 tbsp oil
- 1 cup 5% vinegar

Instructions:

1. In a saucepan, add tomatoes, honey, and salt. Cook for 10 minutes.
2. Add peppers, zucchini, and oil, and cook for 10 minutes more.
3. Add garlic and vinegar, and cook for 10 more minutes.
4. Scoop hot mixture into hot sterilized pint jars, leaving ¼ inch headspace. Remove air bubbles and if necessary, adjust headspace by adding hot mixture. Wipe the rims carefully. Place tops on jars and screw on bands until fingertip tight.
5. Place jars into canner with boiling water, ensuring that they are completely covered with water. Let boil for 20 minutes. Remove jars and cool.

Autumn Pepper Salsa

Prep time: 1 hour 20 minutes (+6 hours)

Cooking time: 20 minutes

Yield: 8 half-pints

Nutrients per 2 tablespoons:

Carbohydrates – 3 g

Fat – 0 g

Protein – 0 g

Sodium – 4 mg

Calories – 13

Ingredients:

- 3 lbs sweet red peppers, seeded, coarsely chopped
- 6 jalapeno peppers, seeded, coarsely chopped
- 1¼ lbs Granny Smith apples, peeled, cut into 1-inch pieces
- 1 lb pears, peeled, cut into 1-inch pieces
- 1 medium onion, cut into 1-inch pieces
- ¾ tsp fennel seed
- 3 tbsp canning salt
- 2 cups white vinegar
- 2 cups sugar
- 1 cup packed brown sugar

Instructions:

1. Process peppers, apples, pears and onion in a food processor until finely chopped. Transfer to a bowl and sprinkle with salt and toss.
2. Allow to stand 6 hours.
3. Drain well.

4. In a Dutch oven, combine pepper mixture, sugars, fennel seed, and vinegar. Bring to a boil, then let simmer, uncovered, 40-45 minutes until slightly thickened.
5. Carefully scoop hot mixture into hot sterilized half-pint jars, leaving ½-inch headspace. Remove air bubbles and if necessary, adjust headspace by adding hot mixture. Wipe the rims carefully. Place tops on jars and screw on bands until fingertip tight.
6. Place jars into canner with boiling water, ensuring that they are completely covered with water. Let boil; for 20 minutes. Remove jars and cool.

Peach Chili Sauce

Prep time: 2 hours 45 minutes

Cooking time: 20 minutes

Yield: 5 pints

Nutrients per 2 tablespoons:

Carbohydrates – 10 g

Protein – 0 g

Sodium – 82 mg

Calories – 40

Ingredients:

- 5 lbs tomatoes
- 1½ lb peaches, chopped
- 3 large sweet onions, chopped
- 3 medium pears, peeled, chopped
- 2 medium green peppers, chopped
- 2 jalapeno peppers, seeded, cut into matchsticks
- 2 celery ribs, chopped
- 1 tsp mixed pickling spices
- 3 cups sugar
- 3 tsp salt
- 2 cups white vinegar

Instructions:

1. In a Dutch oven, bring 2 quarts water to a boil.
2. Place 1-2 tomatoes in boiling water for 30-60. Remove and plunge into ice water. Peel and finely chop tomatoes.
3. Tie pickling spices in a cheesecloth bag.
4. Place all ingredients in the pot. Bring to a boil.
5. Reduce heat and simmer, uncovered, 2-2½ hours until thickened, stirring occasionally. Discard spice bag.
6. Carefully scoop hot mixture into hot sterilized 1-pint jars, leaving ½-inch headspace. Remove air bubbles and if necessary, adjust headspace by adding hot mixture. Wipe the rims carefully. Place tops on jars and screw on bands until fingertip tight.
7. Place jars into canner with boiling water, ensuring that they are completely covered with water. Let boil for 20 minutes. Remove jars and cool.

Pungent Tomato Pear Chutney

Prep time: 45 minutes (+simmering)

Cooking time: 10 minutes

Yield: 5 half-pints

Nutrients per ¼ cup:

Carbohydrates – 22 g

Fat – 0 g

Protein – 1 g

Sodium – 8 mg

Calories – 88

Ingredients:

- 2 lbs pears, peeled, chopped
- 2 lbs tomatoes, peeled, seeded, chopped
- 1 cup finely chopped seeded jalapeno peppers
- 2 cups chopped onions
- 4 tsp minced fresh ginger root
- 1-2 tsp crushed red pepper flakes
- 1 tsp ground mustard
- 1 cup cider vinegar
- 1 cup brown sugar

Instructions:

1. In a Dutch oven, combine all ingredients. Bring to a boil.
2. Reduce heat and simmer for 45-60 minutes, uncovered, until thickened, stirring occasionally.
3. Carefully scoop hot mixture into hot sterilized half-pint jars, leaving ½-inch headspace. Remove air bubbles and if necessary, adjust headspace by adding hot mixture. Wipe the rims carefully. Place tops on jars and screw on bands until fingertip tight.
4. Place jars into canner with boiling water, ensuring that they are completely covered with water. Let boil for 10 minutes. Remove jars and cool.

Fresh-Tasting Ketchup

Prep time: 20 minutes

Cooking time: 95 minutes

Yield: 3½ cups

Nutrients per 2 tablespoons:

Carbohydrates – 10 g

Fat – 0 g

Protein – 0

Sodium – 258 mg

Calories – 40

Ingredients:

- 4 cups chopped seeded peeled tomatoes
- 1 medium green pepper, chopped
- 1 (6 oz) can tomato paste
- 1 medium onion, chopped
- 1 cup sugar
- 1 tbsp salt
- ¼ cup white vinegar

Instructions:

1. In a saucepan, combine first six ingredients and bring to a boil.
2. Reduce heat and simmer, uncovered, until slightly thickened, about 90 minutes.
3. Stir in vinegar and heat through, let boil for 5-7 minutes.
4. Cool to room temperature, and store up to 2 weeks in the refrigerator.

Piquant Chunky Salsa

Prep time: 90 minutes

Cooking time: 15 minutes

Yield: 8 pints

Nutrients per ¼ cup:

Carbohydrates – 6 g

Fat – 0 g

Protein – 1 g

Sodium – 117 mg

Calories – 25

Ingredients:

- 6 lbs tomatoes
- 3 large green peppers, chopped
- 1 large sweet red pepper, chopped
- 4 jalapeno peppers, seeded, chopped
- 2 serrano peppers, seeded, chopped
- 3 large onions, chopped
- 3 garlic cloves, minced
- ½ cup minced fresh cilantro
- 4 tsp ground cumin
- 2 tsp dried oregano
- 1 can (12 oz) tomato paste
- 1 tsp hot pepper sauce
- 2 cups white vinegar
- ½ cup sugar
- ½ cup bottled lemon juice
- 1 tbsp salt

Instructions:

1. In a Dutch oven, bring 2 quarts water to a boil.
2. Place 1-2 tomatoes in boiling water for

30-60 seconds. Remove each tomato and plunge into ice water. Peel and finely chop tomatoes; place in a stockpot.
3. Add remaining ingredients and water to cover. Bring to a boil. Reduce heat and simmer about 30 minutes, uncovered, until slightly thickened.
4. Scoop hot mixture into hot sterilized 1-pint jars, leaving ½ inch headspace. Remove air bubbles and if necessary, adjust headspace by adding hot mixture. Wipe the rims carefully. Place tops on jars and screw on bands until fingertip tight.
5. Place jars into canner with boiling water, ensuring that they are completely covered with water. Let boil for 15 minutes. Remove jars and cool.

Peach Salsa

Prep time: 20 minutes

Cooking time: 3-4 hours (+cooling)

Yield: 11 cups

Nutrients per ¼ cup:

Carbohydrates – 7 g

Fat – 0 g

Protein – 1 g

Sodium – 59 mg

Calories – 28

Ingredients:

- 4 lbs tomatoes, chopped
- 4 jalapeno peppers, seeded, finely chopped
- 1 medium onion, chopped
- ¼ cup minced fresh cilantro
- ½ to ⅔ cup packed brown sugar
- 4 garlic cloves, minced
- 1 tsp salt
- 4 cups chopped peeled fresh peaches, divided
- 1 (6 oz) can tomato paste

Instructions:

1. In a 5-quart slow cooker, mix the first seven ingredients and 2 cups peaches. Cook, covered, on low 3-4 hours or until onion is tender.
2. Stir the remaining peaches and tomato paste into a slow cooker.
3. Let cool, covered, and transfer to covered containers. If freezing, use freezer-safe containers and fill to within ½ inch of tops. Refrigerate up to 7 days or freeze up to 12 months. Before serving thaw frozen salsa in refrigerator.

Grandma's Favourite Salsa

Prep time: 45 minutes

Cooking time: 15 minutes

Yield: 7 pints

Nutrients per ¼ cup:

Carbohydrates – 5 g

Fat – 0 g

Protein – 1 g

Sodium – 300 mg

Calories – 24

Ingredients:

- 2 cups tomato sauce
- 2 cups tomato paste
- 1 cup chopped green pepper
- 2 cups chopped onions
- 3-5 chopped jalapeno peppers, seeded
- 6 garlic cloves, minced
- ½ cup chopped fresh cilantro
- 2 tbsp canning salt
- 2 tsp ground cumin
- 2 tsp pepper
- ⅔ cup white vinegar
- ⅓ cup sugar
- 5 lbs chopped peeled tomatoes, drained

Instructions:

1. In a stockpot, combine all ingredients. Bring to a boil.
2. Reduce heat and let simmer about 20 minutes, uncovered, until vegetables are tender.
3. Scoop hot mixture into hot sterilized 1-pint jars, leaving ½ inch headspace. Remove air bubbles and if necessary, adjust headspace by adding hot mixture. Wipe the rims carefully. Place tops on jars and screw on bands until fingertip tight.
4. Place jars into canner with boiling water, ensuring that they are completely covered with water. Let boil for 15 minutes. Remove jars and cool.

Spaghetti Sauce

Prep time: 90 minutes (+4-5 hours)

Cooking time: 40 minutes

Yield: 9 quarts

Nutrients per ¾ cup:

Carbohydrates – 17 g

Fat – 5 g

Protein – 3 g

Sodium – 614 mg

Calories – 118

Ingredients:

- 25 lbs tomatoes
- 4 large green peppers, seeded
- 4 large onions, cut into wedges
- 2 (24 oz) cans tomato paste
- 8 garlic cloves, minced
- 4 tsp dried oregano
- 2 tsp dried parsley flakes
- 2 tsp dried basil
- 2 tsp crushed red pepper flakes
- 2 tsp Worcestershire sauce
- ¼ cup canola oil
- ⅔ cup sugar
- ¼ cup salt
- 1 cup + 2 tbsp bottled lemon juice
- 2 bay leaves

Instructions:

1. In a Dutch oven, bring 2 quarts water to a boil.
2. Place 1-2 tomatoes in boiling water for 30-60 seconds. Remove each tomato and plunge into ice water. Peel and quarter

tomatoes, then place in a stockpot.

3. Pulse onions and green peppers in batches in a food processor until finely chopped, then transfer to stockpot.
4. Stir in next 11 ingredients.
5. Add water to cover. Bring to a boil.
6. Reduce heat and let simmer for 4-5 hours, stirring occasionally, uncovered.
7. Discard bay leaves.
8. Add 2 tbsp lemon juice to each of 9 hot sterilized 1-quart jars.
9. Scoop hot mixture into jars, leaving ½-inch headspace. Remove air bubbles and if necessary, adjust headspace by adding hot mixture. Wipe the rims carefully. Place tops on jars and screw on bands until fingertip tight.
10. Place jars into canner with boiling water, ensuring that they are completely covered with water. Let boil for 40 minutes. Remove jars and cool.

Green Tomato Salsa

Prep time: 60 minutes (+standing)

Cooking time: 15 minutes

Yield: 8 pints

Nutrients per 2 tablespoons:

Carbohydrates – 9 g

Fat – 0 g

Protein – 0 g

Sodium – 78 mg

Calories – 37

Ingredients:

- 7 lbs green tomatoes
- 3 large green peppers, seedless
- 2 large sweet red peppers, seedless
- 4 large onions
- 2 large red onions
- 2 tbsp celery seed
- 4 tsp mustard seed
- 4 tsp canning salt
- 5 cups cider vinegar
- 4 cups sugar

Instructions:

1. In a food processor, process tomatoes, peppers, and onions until finely chopped.
2. Add salt and mix.
3. Divide mixture between two strainers and place each over a bowl. Let stand for 3 hours.

4. Discard liquid from bowls. Place vegetables in a stockpot and stir in sugar, vinegar, celery and mustard seed. Bring to a boil. Simmer for 30-35 minutes or until thickened, uncovered.
5. Scoop the hot mixture in hot sterilized pint jars, leaving ¼-inch space of the top. Remove air bubbles and if necessary, adjust headspace by adding hot mixture. Wipe the rims carefully. Place tops on jars and screw on bands until fingertip tight.
6. Place jars into canner with simmering water, ensuring that they are completely covered with water. Let boil for 15-17 minutes. Remove jars and cool.

Spicy Carrot Hot Sauce

Prep time: 45 minutes

Cooking time: 10 minutes

Yield: 5 half-pints

Nutrients per 1 teaspoon:

Carbohydrates – 1 g

Fat – 0 g

Protein – 0 g

Sodium – 30 mg

Calories – 3

Ingredients:

- 20 habanero peppers , seeded
- 5 serrano peppers, seeded
- 15 dried Arbol chiles
- 1 large sweet onion, cut into 8 wedges
- 5½ oz carrots, peeled, halved, quartered
- 8 garlic cloves, halved
- 1 cup water
- ¾ cup white vinegar
- ½ cup fresh lime juice
- 3 tsp salt
- 1 tsp coarsely ground pepper

Instructions:

1. In a bowl, cover Arbol chiles with boiling water. Set aside, covered, for 10 minutes, then drain.
2. Fill a 6-quart stockpot three-quarters with water and bring to a boil.
3. Add garlic, carrots, and onion. Cook until soft, about 20-22 minutes. Remove to a bowl.
4. Add peppers to the stockpot and boil for 1 minute; drain.
5. Place lime juice, water, salt, vinegar, and pepper in a blender. Add vegetables and process until smooth. Return to stockpot and bring to a boil.
6. Scoop the hot mixture in hot sterilized 1-pint jars, leaving ¼-inch space of the top. Remove air bubbles and if necessary, adjust headspace by adding hot mixture. Wipe the rims carefully. Place tops on jars and screw on bands until fingertip tight.
7. Place jars into canner, ensuring that they are completely covered with water. Let boil for 10 minutes. Remove jars and cool.

Mild Jalapeno Tomato Salsa

Prep time: 40 minutes (+simmering)

Cooking time: 20 minutes

Yield: 10 pints

Nutrients per 2 tablespoons:

Carbohydrates – 3 g

Fat – 0 g

Protein – 0 g

Sodium – 182 mg

Calories – 14

Ingredients:

- 10½ lbs tomatoes, peeled, quartered
- 3 large onions, chopped
- 4 medium green peppers, chopped
- 1 medium sweet red pepper, chopped
- 1 celery rib, chopped
- 4 jalapeno peppers, seeded, chopped
- 24 oz tomato paste
- ¼ tsp hot pepper sauce
- 1¾ cups white vinegar
- ½ cup sugar
- 15 garlic cloves, minced
- ¼ cup canning salt

Instructions:

1. In a large stockpot, cook tomatoes over medium heat, 20 minutes, uncovered. Drain, reserving 2 cups liquid. Return tomatoes to the pot.

2. Add remaining ingredients and the reserved tomato liquid. Bring to a boil. Reduce heat and let simmer for 1 hour, stirring frequently, uncovered.

3. Scoop the hot mixture in hot sterilized 1-pint jars, leaving ¼-inch space of the top. Remove air bubbles and if necessary, adjust headspace by adding hot mixture. Wipe the rims carefully. Place tops on jars and screw on bands until fingertip tight.

4. Place jars into canner, ensuring that they are completely covered with water. Let boil for 20 minutes. Remove jars and cool.

PICLED TREATS

Pickled Ginger Peaches

Prep time: 20 minutes

Cooking time: 15 minutes

Yield: 12 servings

Nutrients per serving:

Carbohydrates – 19 g

Fat – 0 g

Protein – 1 g

Calories – 78

Ingredients:

- 12 medium peaches, peeled, pitted, quartered
- 2 tsp thinly sliced fresh ginger root
- 6 cinnamon sticks
- 24 whole peppercorns
- 18 whole cloves
- 1 cup white vinegar
- 3 cups sugar
- 1 cup water

Instructions:

1. Place peppercorns, cinnamon sticks, ginger slices, and cloves into 6 hot sterilized pint jars.
2. Add peaches.
3. In a saucepan, bring vinegar, sugar, and water to a boil.
4. Scoop the hot liquid over peaches, leaving ¼-inch of the top. Remove air bubbles and if necessary, adjust headspace by adding hot mixture. Wipe the rims carefully. Place tops on jars and screw on bands until fingertip tight.
5. Place jars into canner, ensuring they are completely covered with water. Let boil for 15-17 minutes. Remove jars and cool.

Watermelon Rind Pickles

Prep time: 45 minutes (+24 hours)

Cooking time: 10 minutes

Yield: 4 pints

Nutrients per ¼ cup:

Carbohydrates – 5 g

Fat – 0 g

Protein – 0 g

Sodium – 96 mg

Calories – 16

Ingredients:

- 8 cups peeled, sliced watermelon rind
- 2 cups white vinegar
- 6 cinnamon sticks, divided
- 1 tsp whole cloves
- 1 tsp whole peppercorns
- 6 cups water
- 1 cup canning salt
- 4 cups sugar

Instructions:

1. Place rind, water, and salt in a large nonreactive bowl. Stir well. Refrigerate for overnight. Rinse and drain well.

2. In a Dutch oven, mix sugar, 2 cinnamon sticks, vinegar, peppercorns, and cloves. Bring to a boil.

3. Add rinds and return to a boil.

4. Reduce heat and let simmer, uncovered, 10 minutes until tender. Discard cinnamon sticks.

5. Carefully scoop the hot mixture into hot sterilized 1-pint jars, leaving ½ inch space of the top. Add the remaining cinnamon stick to each jar. Remove air bubbles and if necessary, adjust headspace by adding hot mixture. Wipe the rims carefully. Place tops on jars and screw on bands until fingertip tight.

6. Place jars into canner, ensuring that they are completely covered with water. Let boil for 10 minutes. Remove jars and cool.

Recipe Notes:

To prepare watermelon rind, remove dark green peel from watermelon rind and throw away.

Pickled Colorful Swiss Chard

Prep time: 10 minutes

Cooking time: 5 minutes

Yield: 8 servings

Nutrients per serving:

Carbohydrates – 11 g

Fat – 0 g

Protein – 2 g

Sodium – 211 mg

Calories – 48

Ingredients:

- 2 bunches rainbow Swiss chard
- 1 small onion, halved, sliced
- 2 tsp mixed pickling spices
- ½ tsp mustard seed
- ½ tsp celery seed
- 1 cup cider vinegar
- 1 cup sugar
- ⅓ cup water

Instructions:

1. Trim leaves from Swiss chard. Cut stems into 2-inch pieces and place in a large heatproof nonreactive bowl.
2. Add pickling spices, onion, celery seed, and mustard seed.
3. In a saucepan, combine vinegar, sugar, and water, and bring to a boil. Cook 1 minute, stirring until sugar dissolves.
4. Pour carefully over chard mixture.
5. Let cool completely. Refrigerate, covered, overnight. Refrigerate up to 3 weeks.

Sandwich Topper Pickled Garlic

Prep time: 20 minutes

Cooking time: 10 minutes

Yield: 3 half-pints

Nutrients per 1 garlic clove:

Carbohydrates – 1 g

Fat – 0 g

Protein – 0 g

Sodium – 30 mg

Calories – 5

Ingredients:

- 3 cups peeled garlic cloves
- 6 whole peppercorns
- 12 coriander seeds
- 3 dried hot chiles, split
- 1 bay leaf, torn into three pieces
- 3 whole allspice
- 2 quarts water
- 1½ cups white wine vinegar
- 1 tbsp sugar
- 1½ tsp canning salt

Instructions:

1. In a saucepan, bring water to a boil.
2. Add garlic and boil 1 minute.
3. Divide peppercorns, coriander, allspice, chiles, and bay leaf among three hot sterilized half-pint jars.
4. Drain garlic and pack into jars to within ½-inch of the top.

5. In a saucepan, mix sugar, salt, and vinegar. Bring to a boil, stirring until sugar and salt are dissolved.
6. Carefully scoop hot liquid over garlic, leaving ½-inch of the top. Remove air bubbles and if necessary, adjust headspace by adding hot mixture. Wipe the rims carefully. Place tops on jars and screw on bands until fingertip tight
7. Place jars into canner with boiling water, ensuring that they are completely covered with water. Let boil for 10 minutes. Remove jars and cool.

Chily Dill Pickles

Prep time: 50 minutes

Cooking time: 15 minutes

Yield: 9 quarts

Nutrients per quart:

Carbohydrates – 1 g

Fat – 0 g

Protein – 1 g

Sodium – 727 mg

Calories – 4

Ingredients:

- 12 lbs pickling cucumbers, halved or quartered lengthwise
- 18 dried hot chilies
- 9 dill sprigs or heads
- 18 garlic cloves
- 11 cups water
- 5 cups white vinegar
- 1 cup canning salt

Instructions:

1. In a stockpot, bring salt, water, and vinegar to a boil. Let boil for 10 minutes.
2. Pack cucumbers into nine hot sterilized quart jars within ½ inch of top.
3. Place two peppers, one dill head, and two garlic cloves in each jar.
4. Carefully scoop the hot liquid over cucumbers, leaving ¼-inch space of the top. Remove air bubbles and if necessary, adjust headspace by adding hot mixture. Wipe the rims carefully. Place tops on jars and screw on bands until fingertip tight.
5. Place jars into canner, ensuring that they are completely covered with water. Let boil for 15 minutes. Remove jars and cool.

Bread and Butter Pickles

Prep time: 45 minutes (+3 hours)

Cooking time: 10 minutes per batch

Yield: 11 pints

Nutrients per ¼ cup:

Carbohydrates – 15 g

Fat – 0 g

Protein – 1 g

Sodium – 645 mg

Calories – 60

Ingredients:

- 20 cups sliced cucumbers
- 3 cups sliced onions
- 1 medium green pepper, sliced
- 1 medium sweet red pepper, sliced
- 5 cups ice water
- ½ cup canning salt
- 6 cups sugar
- 6 cups white vinegar
- 3 tbsp mustard seed
- 3 tsp celery seed
- 1½ tsp ground turmeric
- ¼ tsp ground cloves

Instructions:

1. Place onions, cucumbers, and peppers in a large bowl.
2. In another large bowl, mix salt and ice water. Pour over vegetables and let stand 3 hours.
3. Rinse vegetables and drain well. Pack vegetables into eleven hot 1-pint jars to within ½-inch of the top.
4. In a Dutch oven, bring sugar, vinegar, mustard seed, celery seed, turmeric and cloves to a boil.
5. Carefully scoop the hot liquid over vegetables, leaving ¼-inch space of the top. Remove air bubbles and if necessary, adjust headspace by adding hot mixture. Wipe the rims carefully. Place tops on jars and screw on bands until fingertip tight.
6. Place jars into canner, ensuring that they are completely covered with water. Let boil for 10 minutes. Remove jars and cool.

Sweet Pickles

Prep time: 60 minutes (+ 3 hours)

Cooking time: 10 minutes

Yield: 4 pints

Nutrients per ¼ cup:

Carbohydrates – 8 g

Fat – 0 g

Protein – 0 g

Sodium – 175 mg

Calories – 35

Ingredients:

- 9 cups sliced pickling cucumbers
- 1 large sweet onion, thinly sliced
- ¼ cup canning salt
- 12 garlic cloves, crushed
- 1 tsp celery seed
- 2 tbsp mustard seed
- ½ tsp whole peppercorns
- 4 bay leaves
- 1 cup sugar
- 1 cup white vinegar
- 1 cup water
- ½ cup cider vinegar

Instructions:

1. In a nonreactive bowl, combine onion, cucumbers, and salt. Mix well and cover with crushed ice. Let stand for 3 hours. Drain and rinse thoroughly.

2. In a Dutch oven, combine mustard and celery seed, sugar, peppercorns, water, and vinegars. Bring to a boil. Stir until sugar dissolves.

3. Add cucumber mixture and bring to a boil, stirring occasionally. Simmer for 4-5 minutes, uncovered.

4. Carefully scoop hot mixture into four hot sterilized 1-pint jars, leaving ½-inch headspace.

5. Add 1 bay leaf and 3 garlic cloves to each jar. Remove air bubbles and if necessary, adjust headspace by adding hot mixture. Wipe the rims carefully. Place tops on jars and screw on bands until fingertip tight.

6. Place jars into canner with simmering water, ensuring that they are completely covered with water. Let boil for 10 minutes. Remove jars and cool.

Pickled Brussels Sprouts

Prep time: 30 minutes

Cooking time: 10 minutes

Yield: 6 pints

Nutrients per ¼ cup:

Carbohydrates – 3 g

Fat – 0 g

Protein – 1 g

Sodium – 11 mg

Calories – 14

Ingredients:

- 3 lbs fresh Brussels sprouts, halved
- 1 medium sweet red pepper, finely chopped
- 6 garlic cloves, halved
- 1 medium onion, thinly sliced
- 2 tsp crushed red pepper flakes
- 1 tbsp celery seed
- 1 tbsp whole peppercorns
- 3 tbsp canning salt
- ½ cup sugar
- 2½ cups white vinegar
- 2½ cups water

Instructions:

1. Fill a Dutch oven three-fourths full with water; bring to a boil.
2. Add Brussels sprouts in batches, cooking, uncovered, 4 minutes until tender-crisp.
3. With a slotted spoon remove and drop into ice water. Drain and pat dry.

4. Pack Brussels sprouts into six hot 1-pint jars.
5. Divide garlic and pepper flakes among jars.
6. In a large saucepan, bring remaining ingredients to a boil.
7. Carefully scoop the hot liquid over Brussels sprouts, leaving ¼-inch space of the top. Remove air bubbles and if necessary, adjust headspace by adding hot mixture. Wipe the rims carefully. Place tops on jars and screw on bands until fingertip tight.
8. Place jars into canner with simmering water, ensuring that they are completely covered with water. Let boil for 10 minutes. Remove jars and cool.

Pickled Green Beans

Prep time: 20 minutes

Cooking time: 10 minutes

Yield: 4 pints

Nutrients per 8 green beans:

Carbohydrates – 2 g

Fat – 0 g

Protein – 1 g

Sodium – 83 mg

Calories – 9

Ingredients:

- 1¾ lbs fresh green beans
- 1 tsp cayenne pepper
- 4 garlic cloves, peeled
- 4 tsp dill seed
- 2½ cups water
- 2½ cups white vinegar
- ¼ cup canning salt

Instructions:

1. Pack beans into four hot 1-pint jars to within ½-inch of the top.
2. Add dill seed, cayenne, and garlic to jars.
3. In a large saucepan, bring the vinegar, water, and salt to a boil.
4. Carefully scoop the hot liquid over beans, leaving ¼-inch space of the top. Remove air bubbles and if necessary, adjust headspace by adding hot mixture. Wipe the rims carefully. Place tops on jars and screw on bands until fingertip tight.
5. Place jars into canner with boiling water, ensuring that they are completely covered with water. Let boil for 10 minutes. Remove jars and cool.

Christmas Pickled Morsels

Prep time: 10 minutes

Cooking time: 25 minutes

Yield: 6½ quarts

Nutrients per ¼ cup:

Carbohydrates – 25 g

Fat – 0 g

Protein – 1 g

Sodium – 55 mg

Calories – 99

Ingredients:

- 1 gallon whole dill pickles
- 3-4 jalapeno peppers, chopped
- 1 tbsp whole cloves
- 1 lb whole candied cherries
- 3 jars pearl onions, drained
- 4-5 garlic cloves, minced
- 11¼ cups sugar
- 1 cup white vinegar
- 1 tbsp mustard seed
- 4-5 whole cinnamon sticks
- 1 tsp olive oil

Instructions:

1. Drain pickles, reserving juice.
2. Cut pickles into ½-inch slices and set aside.
3. In a stockpot, combine vinegar, sugar, mustard seed, peppers, cloves, garlic, cinnamon sticks, and pickle juice.

4. Cook over medium heat for 10 minutes, stirring until sugar is dissolved.
5. Bring to a boil, then reduce to a simmer. Cook, uncovered, for 10 minutes.
6. Remove from heat and let cool slightly. Discard cinnamon sticks.
7. In a large bowl, combine onions, cherries, and pickle slices. Pour liquid over pickle mixture. Stir in oil.
8. Refrigerate, covered, for 48 hours, stirring occasionally.
9. Divide mixture among sterilized jars. Store in the refrigerator up to 30 days, covered.

Pickled Sweet Banana Peppers

Prep time: 30 minutes

Cooking time: 15 minutes

Yield: 5 pints

Nutrients per 1 ounce:

Carbohydrates – 3 g

Fat – 0 g

Protein – 0 g

Sodium – 15 mg

Calories – 13

Ingredients:

- 8 banana peppers, seedless, cut into strips
- 5 large sweet red peppers, seedless, cut into strips
- 1 medium onion, thinly sliced
- 8 garlic cloves, peeled
- 2 tsp canning salt
- 1¼ cups sugar
- 4 tsp canola oil
- 2½ cups water
- 2½ cups white vinegar

Instructions:

1. Pack peppers into 5 hot sterilized 1-pint jars to within ½ inch of the top.
2. Divide the garlic, onion, and oil among jars.
3. In a large saucepan, bring water, sugar, vinegar, and salt to a boil.
4. Carefully scoop hot liquid over pepper mixture, leaving ¼-inch headspace. Remove air bubbles and if necessary, adjust headspace by adding hot mixture. Wipe the rims carefully. Place tops on jars and screw on bands until fingertip tight.
5. Place jars into canner with boiling water, make sure that they are covered with water. Let boil for 15 minutes. Remove jars and let cool.

Tangy Pickled Mushrooms

Prep time: 50 minutes

Cooking time: 20 minutes

Yield: 8 pints

Nutrients per ¼ cup:

Carbohydrates – 2 g

Fat – 1 g

Protein – 1 g

Sodium – 35 mg

Calories – 18

Ingredients:

- 5 lbs small fresh mushrooms, sliced
- 2 large onions, halved, sliced
- 3 garlic cloves, minced
- 1½ tsp pepper
- ¼ tsp dried tarragon
- 2 cups white vinegar
- 1½ cups canola oil
- ¼ cup sugar
- 2 tbsp canning salt

Instructions:

1. In a stockpot, bring all ingredients to a boil. Reduce heat and simmer, uncovered, 10 minutes.

2. Carefully scoop hot mixture into hot sterilized 1-pint jars, leaving ½-inch headspace. Remove air bubbles and if necessary, adjust headspace by adding hot mixture. Wipe the rims carefully. Place tops on jars and screw on bands until fingertip tight

3. Place jars into canner with boiling water, ensuring that they are completely covered with water. Let boil for 20 minutes. Remove jars and cool.

Flavor-Packed Pickled Red Grapes

Prep time: 35 minutes

Cooking time: 10 minutes

Yield: 4 pints

Nutrients per ¼ cup:

Carbohydrates – 8 g

Fat – 0 g

Protein – 0 g

Sodium – 7 mg

Calories – 32

Ingredients:

- 5 cups seedless red grapes
- 4 jalapeno peppers, seeded, sliced
- 2 cinnamon sticks, halved
- 2 tbsp fresh minced ginger root
- 2 tsp coriander seeds
- 4 whole star anise
- 2 tsp mustard seed
- 1½ tsp canning salt
- 2 cups packed brown sugar
- 2 cups white wine vinegar
- 1 cup water
- 1 cup dry red wine

Instructions:

1. Pack grapes into four hot sterilized 1-pint jars to within 1½ inch of the top.
2. Divide ginger, jalapenos, star anise, cinnamon, coriander and mustard seeds among jars.
3. In a saucepan, combine vinegar, brown sugar, water, wine and canning salt. Bring to a boil and cook until liquid is reduced about to 3 cups, 15-18 minutes.
4. Carefully scoop hot liquid over the grape mixture, leaving ½-inch of the top. Remove air bubbles and if necessary, adjust headspace by adding hot mixture. Wipe the rims carefully. Place tops on jars and screw on bands until fingertip tight
5. Place jars into canner with boiling water, ensuring that they are completely covered with water. Let boil for 10 minutes. Remove jars and cool.

Pickled Sweet-Sour Squash

Prep time: 20 minutes (+standing)

Cooking time: 10 minutes (+chilling)

Yield: 4 cups

Nutrients per ½ cup:

Carbohydrates – 30 g

Fat – 0 g

Protein – 1 g

Sodium – 225 mg

Calories – 123

Ingredients:

- 3 small yellow squash, thinly sliced
- 1 large sweet red pepper, cut into ¼-inch strips
- 1 medium onion, chopped
- ¾ cup white vinegar
- ¾ tsp mustard seed
- ¾ tsp celery seed
- ¼ tsp ground mustard
- 1 tbsp salt
- 1 cup sugar

Instructions:

1. Place pepper, squash, and onion in a bowl. Sprinkle with salt and let stand for 1 hour.
2. In a saucepan, combine the remaining ingredients. Bring to a boil. Stir until sugar dissolves.
3. Add vegetables and return to a boil.
4. Remove from heat and cool completely.
5. Transfer to a covered container and refrigerate for 4 days before serving. May be stored in refrigerator up to 3 weeks.

Spiced Pickled Beets

Prep time: 85 minutes

Cooking time: 35 minutes

Yield: 4 pints

Nutrients per ¼ cup:

Carbohydrates – 12 g

Fat – 0 g

Protein – 1 g

Sodium – 44 mg

Calories – 53

Ingredients:

- 3 lbs fresh, small beets
- 2 cups sugar
- 2 cups water
- 2 cups cider vinegar
- 2 cinnamon sticks
- 1 tsp whole cloves
- 1 tsp whole allspice

Instructions:

1. Scrub beets and detruncate tops to 1 inch. Put in a Dutch oven and cover with water. Bring to a boil.
2. Reduce heat and let simmer, covered, until tender, 25-35 minutes.
3. Remove from water and let cool. Peel beets and cut into fourths.
4. Place beets in a Dutch oven with vinegar, sugar, and water.
5. Wrap cinnamon sticks, cloves, and allspice in a double thickness of cheesecloth.Add to beet mixture.

6. Bring to a boil, then reduce heat and cover. Let simmer 10 minutes. Discard spice bag.
7. Pack beets into four hot sterilized 1-pint jars to within ½-inch of the top.
8. Carefully scoop the hot liquid over beets, leaving ¼-inch space of the top. Remove air bubbles and if necessary, adjust headspace by adding hot mixture. Wipe the rims carefully. Place tops on jars and screw on bands until fingertip tight.
9. Place jars into canner with boiling water, ensuring that they are completely covered with water. Let boil for 35 minutes. Remove jars and cool.

Giardiniera

Prep time: 60 minutes

Cooking time: 10 minutes

Yield: 10 pints

Nutrients per ¼ cup:

Carbohydrates – 3 g

Fat – 0 g

Protein – 0 g

Sodium – 88 mg

Calories – 15

Ingredients:

- 2 small cauliflowers, broken into florets
- 4 celery ribs, cut into ½-inch slices
- 4 large carrots, sliced
- 1¼ lb pearl onions, peeled, trimmed
- 4 serrano peppers, seeded, thinly sliced
- 4 large sweet red peppers, cut into ½-inch strips
- 6 cups white vinegar
- 3½ cups sugar
- 3 cups water
- 4½ tsp canning salt
- 1 tbsp dried oregano
- 1 tbsp fennel seed
- 10 bay leaves
- 20 whole peppercorns
- 10 garlic cloves, thinly sliced

Instructions:

1. In a stockpot, combine sugar, vinegar, water, oregano, fennel seed and canning salt. Bring to a boil.

2. Add carrots, cauliflower, onions, and celery. Return to a boil.
3. Remove from heat and add peppers.
4. Carefully scoop hot mixture into hot sterilized 1-pint jars, leaving ½-inch headspace.
5. Add a few slices of garlic, a bay leaf, and 2 peppercorns to each jar. Remove air bubbles and if necessary, adjust headspace by adding hot mixture. Wipe the rims carefully. Place tops on jars and screw on bands until fingertip tight.
6. Place jars into canner with boiling water, ensuring that they are completely covered with water. Let boil for 10 minutes. Remove jars and cool.

Sweet and Sour Pickled Zucchini Slices

Prep time: 60 minutes (+2 hours)

Cooking time: 10 minutes

Yield: 6 pints

Nutrients per ¼ cup:

Carbohydrates – 3 g

Fat – 0 g

Protein – 0 g

Sodium – 87 mg

Calories – 12

Ingredients:

- 3 lbs thinly sliced zucchini
- 1 large onion, halved, thinly sliced
- 1 tbsp mustard seed
- 1½ tsp ground turmeric
- ⅓ cup canning salt
- 4½ cups white vinegar
- 3 cups sugar

Instructions:

1. In a large nonreactive bowl, sprinkle zucchini and onion with salt and toss to coat.
2. Cover with water and let stand at room temperature for 2 hours. Drain and rinse thoroughly.
3. In a 6-quart stockpot, combine the remaining ingredients. Bring to a boil. Stir until sugar is fully dissolved.
4. Reduce heat and simmer 5 minutes to allow flavors to blend.
5. Add zucchini mixture and return to a boil, stirring occasionally.
6. Reduce heat and let simmer, uncovered, 4-5 minutes until heated through.
7. Carefully scoop hot mixture into hot sterilized 1-pint jars, leaving ½-inch headspace. Remove air bubbles and if necessary, adjust headspace by adding hot mixture. Wipe the rims carefully. Place tops on jars and screw on bands until fingertip tight
8. Place jars into canner with boiling water, ensuring that they are completely covered with water. Let boil for 10 minutes. Remove jars and cool.

CONCLUSION

Thank you for reading this book and having the patience to try the recipes.

I do hope that you have had as much enjoyment reading and experimenting with the meals as I have had writing the book.

If you would like to leave a comment, you can do so at the Order section->Digital orders, in your account.

Stay safe and healthy!

Recipe Index

A

Apple-Walnut Maple Confiture 39
Apricot Amaretto Jam 18
Autumn Pepper Salsa 45

B

Baked Garlic Ghee Chicken Breast 55
Blueberry Cinnamon Jam 20
Bread and Butter Pickles 61

C

Candy Apple Jelly 30
Canned Zucchini Salad 44
Caramel Apple Jam 28
Carrot Pineapple Pear Jam 21
Chily Dill Pickles 60
Christmas Cranberry Jam 29
Christmas Pickled Morsels 65
Chunky Peach Spread 38
Crispy Oven Roasted Salmon 50
Cucumber Jelly 33

F

Flavor-Packed Pickled Red Grapes 68
Fresh-Tasting Ketchup 48

G

Giardiniera 71
Ginger Pear Freezer Jam 25
Glazed Carrots 35
Grandma's Favourite Salsa 51
Green Tomato Jam 22
Green Tomato Salsa 53

L

Lemon Marmalade 36
Lime Mint Jelly 31

P

Peach Chili Sauce 46
Pickled Brussels Sprouts 63
Pickled Colorful Swiss Chard 58
Pickled Ginger Peaches 56
Pickled Green Beans 64
Pickled Sweet Banana Peppers 66
Pickled Sweet-Sour Squash 69
Pina Colada Zucchini Jam 26
Pineapple Rhubarb Jam 23
Piquant Chunky Salsa 49
Plum Cranberry Walnut Conserve 34
Plum Orange Jam 24
Pungent Tomato Pear Chutney 47

R

Raisin Pear Chutney 37
Raspberry Peach Jam 19
Rhubarb Cherry Chutney 42

S

Sandwich Topper Pickled Garlic 59
Spaghetti Sauce 52
Spiced Cran-Apple and Grape Confiture 41
Spiced Pickled Beets 70
Spicy Carrot Hot Sauce 54
Spicy Roasted Beet Marmalade 40
Strawberry Freezer Jam 27
Sweet and Sour Pickled Zucchini Slices 72
Sweet Pickles 62

T

Tangy Pickled Mushrooms 67
Tomato Lemon Confiture 43

W

Watermelon Jelly 32
Watermelon Rind Pickles 57

Conversion Tables

VOLUME EQUIVALENTS (LIQUID)

US STANDARD	US STANDARD (OUNCES)	METRIC
2 tablespoons	1 fl. oz.	30 mL
¼ cup	2 fl. oz.	60 mL
½ cup	4 fl. oz.	120 mL
1 cup	8 fl. oz.	240mL
1½ cups	12 fl. oz.	355 mL
2 cups or 1 pint	16 fl. oz.	475 mL
4 cups or 1 quart	32 fl. oz.	1 L
1 gallon	128 fl. oz.	4 L

OVEN TEMPERATURES

FAHRENHEIT (°F)	CELSIUS (°C) APPROXIMATE
250 °F	120 °C
300 °F	150 °C
325 °F	165 °C
350 °F	180 °C
375 °F	190 °C
400 °F	200 °C
425 °F	220 °C
450 °F	230 °C

VOLUME EQUIVALENTS (LIQUID)

US STANDARD	METRIC (APPROXIMATE)
⅛ teaspoon	0.5 mL
¼ teaspoon	1 mL
½ teaspoon	2 mL
⅔ teaspoon	4 mL
1 teaspoon	5 mL
1 tablespoon	15 mL
¼ cup	59 mL
⅓ cup	79 mL
½ cup	118 mL
⅔ cup	156 mL
¾ cup	177 mL
1 cup	235 mL
2 cups or 1 pint	475 mL
3 cups	700 mL
4 cups or 1 quart	1 L
½ gallon	2 L
1 gallon	4 L

WEIGHT EQUIVALENTS

US STANDARD	METRIC (APPROXIMATE)
½ ounce	15 g
1 ounce	30 g
2 ounces	60 g
4 ounces	115 g
8 ounces	225 g
12 ounces	340 g
16 ounces or 1 pound	455 g